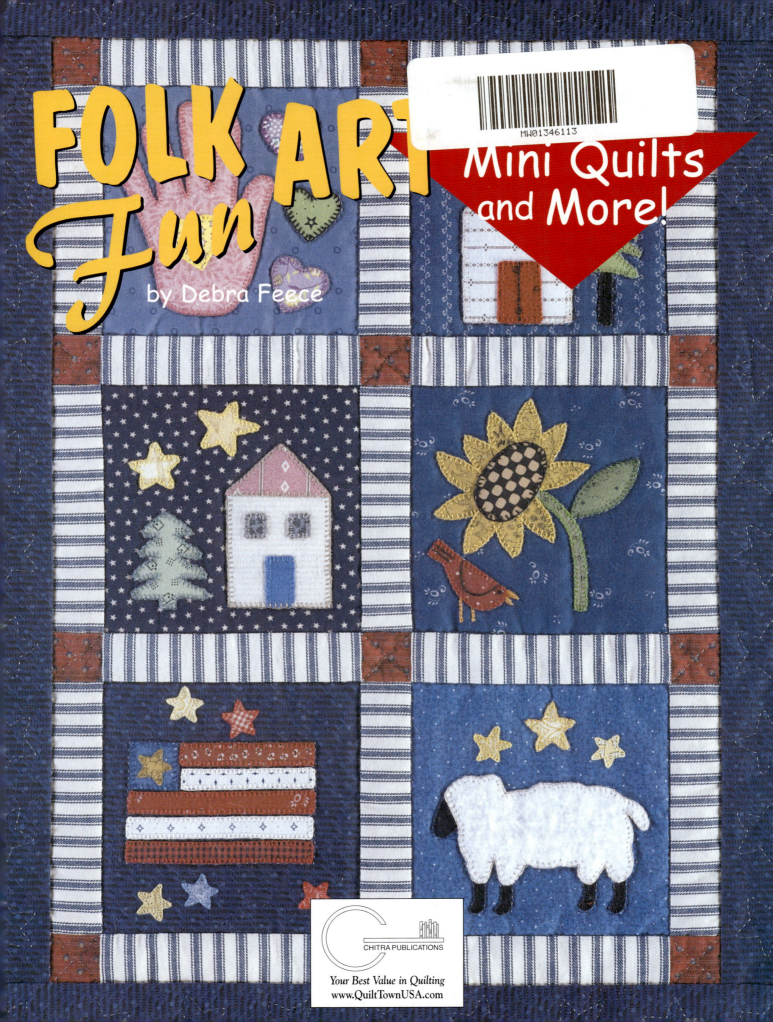

Introduction

When I volunteered to design a series of Folk Art blocks for *Miniature Quilts* magazine, I had no idea it would develop into a book. Stitching the little sampler blocks and assembling them into finished quilts was fun. When the series was finished, I thought that was the end of it. Then we started getting letters from readers telling us how much they enjoyed the series. Some sent photos of their finished quilts, and many asked for more designs.

So, upon encouragement from my friends at Chitra Publications, I set about designing more blocks. With the exception of "Animal Stack," all of the quilt patterns in this book contain 5" finished blocks, which means they're interchangeable. These designs are easy and quick to make using fusible web and a blanket stitch.

I hope my designs inspire you to stitch your own mini Folk Art quilts and that you have as much fun making yours as I had making mine.

Acknowledgements

I'd like to thank the Apple Wagon in Tunkhannock, Pennsylvania, and Lily Pad Gifts in Montrose, Pennsylvania, for their generosity in allowing me to borrow many of the antiques and collectibles that appear in this book.

Contents

- 3   Mountain Cabin
- 3   Field Trip Moose
- 4   Animal Stack
- 6   Mini Baskets
- 8   Miss Kitty's Favorite
- 10   Summer Days
- 12   Wild Things
- 14   Trio of Angels
- 16   Christmas Pillows
- 18   Checkers Anyone?
- 19   Checkers Pouch
- 20   Folk Art Sampler
- 20   Folk Art in Plaid
- 24   Caitie's Cats
- 26   Old Cat
- 31   General Directions
- 32   Embroidery Stitches

Mountain Cabin AND Field Trip Moose

When our family lived in beautiful New Hampshire for almost 3 years, my 2 daughters and I were beginning to think we'd never see a moose. The day Caitlin decided she would rather go antiquing with me than on another school field trip, we saw one. We watched him for about 20 minutes as he stood drinking from a puddle in a field. Just 2 weeks later, Marissa decided she'd rather go shopping than on a field trip, so off we went. You guessed it, we saw a moose! He crossed the road in front of our car. I made "**Field Trip Moose**" to commemorate those events. "**The Mountain Cabin**" quilt is a perfect companion in a framed display.

Mountain Cabin

BLOCK SIZE: 5" square

MATERIALS
- Tea-dyed muslin or mottled tan at least 7" square (To tea dye fabric, see page 5.)
- Piece of gray at least 5" x 7"
- Yellow print scrap
- Red print scrap
- Black print scrap
- Red print scrap
- 2 gold print scraps
- Piece of muslin at least 14" x 21"
- 9" square of thin batting
- Embroidery floss to match or contrast with the fabrics
- Frame for a 5 1/2" picture
- Piece of cardboard at least 6" square
- Fusible Web

CUTTING
Trace the Mountain Cabin and Star patterns (on page 32), on the paper side of the fusible web. Cut the shapes out on the line. Set the tall cabin piece and the short cabin piece aside. Fuse the remaining shapes to the wrong side of the appropriate fabrics and cut them out on the lines.

For the appliqués:
- Cut 1: roof, black print
- Cut 3: windows, yellow print
- Cut 1: door, red print
- Cut 2: stars, gold prints

Also:
- Cut 1: 7" square, tea-dyed muslin
- Cut 1: 12" square, muslin
- Cut 1: 9" square, muslin
- Cut 6: 3/4" x 5" strips, muslin
- Cut 7: 1" x 5" strips, gray

DIRECTIONS
- Sew a 1" x 5" gray strip to a 3/4" x 5" muslin strip along their length.
- Sew a 3/4" x 5" muslin strip to the other long side of the gray strip. Continue adding strips, alternating gray and muslin to make a pieced panel at least 3 1/4" wide. NOTE: *When joining the strips, don't worry about sewing straight or about sewing a perfect 1/4" seam allowance. Sew the gray strips so they vary in width (from 5/16" to 1/2") and the muslin is very narrow (from 1/16" to 1/8" wide).*
- Trim the seam allowances to 1/8" and press all of them toward the gray. The pressing is important because it makes the muslin recede, giving the appearance of chinking.
- Fuse the tall cabin piece to the wrong side of the pieced panel, making sure the top and bottom edges are on a gray strip. Fuse the short cabin piece in the same manner, making sure the chinking strips won't be in alignment.
- Cut the pieces out on the lines.
- Arrange the cabin pieces, roof, door, *(continued on page 7)*

These designs are perfect for anyone longing for a mountain getaway.

Animal Stack

Have fun stitching this folksy group of friends.

One of my favorite tales, *The Bremen Town Musicians*, inspired **"Animal Stack"**. I've always enjoyed this story of downtrodden animals hoisting each other up to a window to scare the robbers away. My daughter Marissa drew some of these animals and lent her "expert" advice with color. I chose to fuse and stitch the border triangles because I liked the look of the background fabric extending beyond the triangles.

QUILT SIZE: 12" x 16"

MATERIALS
- Fat quarter (18" x 22") white with dots for the background
- Assorted prints for the animals
- Bright blue print scrap for the bird
- Black scrap for the sheep's face and feet
- Assorted brown and rust print scraps including prints, plaids, stripes, and checks for the border
- 14" x 18" piece of backing fabric
- 14" x 18" piece of thin batting
- Embroidery floss to match or contrast with the fabrics, including orange for the bird's feet, and black for the border triangles
- Fusible Web

CUTTING
Trace the patterns on the paper side of the fusible web. Cut the shapes out slightly beyond the lines. Fuse the shapes to the wrong side of the appropriate fabrics and cut them out on the lines.
For the appliqués:
- Cut 1 each: horse, sheep, dog, and cat, assorted prints
- Cut 1: bird, bright blue print
- Cut 20: triangles, assorted brown and rust prints, plaids, stripes, and checks

Also:
- Cut 1: 13" x 17" rectangle, white with dots
- Cut 2: 1 1/4" x 17" strips, gold print, for the binding
- Cut 2: 1 1/4" x 13" strips, gold print, for the binding

DIRECTIONS
- Referring to the quilt photo, arrange the animals on the 13" x 17" white rectangle. Place the bird 1/8" above the cat's tail. Measure the sides, top, and bottom and adjust the arrangement as necessary to keep it centered.
- Fuse the pieces in place.
- Stitch around the bird with a small blanket stitch, using one strand of matching embroidery floss.
- Stitch around the animals using 2 strands of matching or contrasting embroidery floss.
- Stitch 2 little bird legs with a straight stitch, using one strand of orange embroidery floss.

- Place the assorted triangles on the background rectangle, making a frame around the animals. Measure and rearrange as necessary to keep the frame straight and the animals centered within it.
- Fuse the triangles in place.
- Stitch around the triangles with a small blanket stitch, using 2 strands of black embroidery floss.
- Press the quilt on the wrong side.
- Trim the edges of the rectangle 1" beyond the points of the triangles.

Full-Size Patterns for Animal Stack

- Finish the quilt as described in the *General Directions*, using the 1 1/4"-wide gold print strips and Binding Method #2.

Tea-dyeing Fabric

Bring a large pot of water to a boil. Turn off the burner and place several tea bags in the water. Let them steep until the water is a nice dark color. Remove the tea bags and place the muslin in the water.

For a light tint, immerse the fabric for only a brief moment. The longer you leave the fabric in the tea, the darker the color will be. NOTE: *Tea-dyed fabric looks slightly darker when wet.* Remove the fabric from the tea when desired and rinse it with cold water. Wring it out and hang it until it's almost dry. Press the fabric to finish drying and remove the wrinkles.

Mini Baskets

Basket designs appeal to me. After I made a full-size needleturn appliqué block for *Traditional Quiltworks* magazine, I thought "this would be so cute in a miniature quilt." **"Mini Baskets"** was fun from shopping for the fabrics to stitching the binding on.

QUILT SIZE: 17 1/2" square
BLOCK SIZE: 5" square

MATERIALS
- Fat quarter (18" x 22") light print
- 4 assorted blue print scraps, each at least 4" square, for the baskets
- Red polka dot at least 12" square
- Bright yellow scrap
- 2 green prints, each at least 4" square
- 1/3 yard blue plaid
- 20" square of backing fabric
- 20" square of thin batting
- Fusible Web

CUTTING
Trace the Mini Baskets patterns (on page 32) on the paper side of the fusible web. Cut the shapes out slightly beyond the lines. Fuse the shapes to the wrong side of the appropriate fabrics and cut them out on the lines.

For the appliqués:
- Cut 1: basket, from each blue print scrap
- Cut 4: flowers, red polka dot
- Cut 4: flower centers, bright yellow
- Cut 8: small leaves, from each green print
- Cut 4: large leaves, from each green print

Also:
- Cut 4: 6" squares, light print
- Cut 7: 4" squares, light print
- Cut 7: 4" squares, red polka dot
- Cut 4: 1 1/2" squares, red polka dot
- Cut 2: 1 1/4" x 40" strips, blue plaid, for the binding
- Cut 2: 1 1/2" x 17 1/2" strips, blue plaid
- Cut 2: 1 1/2" x 15 1/2" strips, blue plaid
- Cut 2: 1 1/2" x 13 1/2" strips, blue plaid
- Cut 3: 1 1/2" x 11 1/2" strips, blue plaid
- Cut 2: 1 1/2" x 5 1/2" strips, blue plaid

DIRECTIONS
- Center a blue print basket on a 6" light print square. Fuse it in place.
- Referring to the photo, place a red polka dot flower and a bright yellow flower center on the basket. Place 2 large and 4 small matching green print leaves on the basket. Fuse them in place.
- Stitch around the basket with a small blanket stitch using 2 strands of matching or contrasting embroidery floss. Stitch around the flower, flower center, and leaves using one strand of floss. Make 4.
- Press the blocks on the wrong side.
- Trim each block to 5 1/2" square, keeping the basket centered.
- Lay out the blocks in 2 rows of 2. Place the 1 1/2" x 5 1/2" blue plaid strips between the blocks in the vertical rows. Stitch the blocks and strips into 2 vertical rows.
- Stitch the 1 1/2" x 11 1/2" blue plaid strips between the vertical rows and on each side.
- Stitch the 1 1/2" x 13 1/2" blue plaid strips to the top and bot-

tom. Set the quilt aside.
- Draw diagonal lines from corner to corner on the wrong side of each 4" light print square. Draw horizontal and vertical lines through the centers.
- Place a marked square on a 4" red polka dot square, right sides together. Sew 1/4" away from the diagonal lines on both sides. Make 7.
- Cut the squares on the drawn lines to yield 56 pieced squares. You will use 52. Press the seam allowances open then trim them to 1/8".
- Trim each pieced square to 1 1/2".
- Lay out 13 pieced squares, as shown. Stitch them together to make a side border. Make 2.
- Referring to the photo for color placement, stitch the side borders to the sides of the quilt.

- Lay out 13 pieced squares, as shown. Stitch them together. Stitch a 1 1/2" red polka dot square to each end to make a border. Make 2.

- Stitch the borders to the top and bottom of the quilt.
- Stitch the 1 1/2" x 15 1/2" blue plaid strips to the sides of the quilt.
- Stitch the 1 1/2" x 17 1/2" blue plaid strips to the top and bottom of the quilt.
- Finish the quilt as described in the *General Directions*, using the 1 1/4" x 40" blue plaid strips and Binding Method #1.

NOTE: *The sashing and border quilting design I used for Folk Art Baskets is provided on page 32. Cut the shape out of paper. Align the straight edge of the paper with one edge of the sashing or border strip and trace the curved edge. Draw leaves on the inner curves. Trace the appliqué flower pattern on paper and cut it out. Trace it on the sashing at each corner of the blocks.*

Mountain Cabin (continued from page 3)

windows, and stars on the 7" tea-dyed square. Fuse them in place. Turn the square over and press it again on the wrong side.
- Stitch around the cabin, roof, and door with a small blanket stitch, using 2 strands of matching or contrasting embroidery floss.
- Stitch around the windows and stars with one strand of matching or contrasting embroidery floss.
- Press the block on the wrong side.
- Measure the opening in the back of the frame. Trim the block 1/4" larger than that measurement.
- Layer the 9" square of muslin, batting, and the block, right side up. Baste the layers. Quilt as desired.

Framing the Block:
- Measure the qulted block and trim it to equal the measurement of the opening in the back of the frame.
- Cut a square of cardboard that same measurement.
- Center and pin the block on the 12" square of muslin. Baste the block to the muslin 1/8" from the edge of the block on all sides.
- Place the block right side down and center the cardboard on it. Fold the sides of the muslin over the cardboard toward the center. Check to make sure the block is centered on the cardboard. Thread a needle with a long piece of thread and whipstitch the edges of the muslin together, as shown, pulling the thread tight.
- Fold the top and bottom edges of the muslin over the cardboard, checking to be sure the block is centered. Whipstitch the edges together, as before.
- Place the Mountain Cabin in the frame. Secure it in place.

Field Trip Moose (shown on page 3)

BLOCK SIZE: 5" square

MATERIALS
- Navy plaid at least 5" square
- Tea-dyed muslin or mottled tan at least 7" square (To tea dye fabric, see page 5.)
- Piece of muslin at least 12" x 21"
- 9" square of thin batting
- Navy embroidery floss
- Frame for a 5 1/2" picture
- Piece of cardboard at least 6" square
- Fusible Web

CUTTING
Trace the Moose pattern (on page 32) on the paper side of the fusible web. Cut the shape out on the line. Fuse the shape to the wrong side of the appropriate fabric and cut it out on the line.
For the appliqué:
- Cut 1: moose, navy plaid
Also:
- Cut 1: 7" square, tea-dyed muslin
- Cut 1: 12" square, muslin
- Cut 1: 9" square, muslin

DIRECTIONS
- Center the moose on the 7" square of tea-dyed muslin. Fuse it in place.
- Stitch around the moose with a small blanket stitch, using 2 strands of navy embroidery floss.
- Press the block on the wrong side.
- Measure the opening in the back of the frame. Trim the Moose block 1/4" larger than that measurement.
- Layer the 9" square of muslin, batting, and the Moose block, right side up. Baste the layers. Quilt as desired.
- Frame the block as described in Mountain Cabin.

Miss Kitty's Favorite

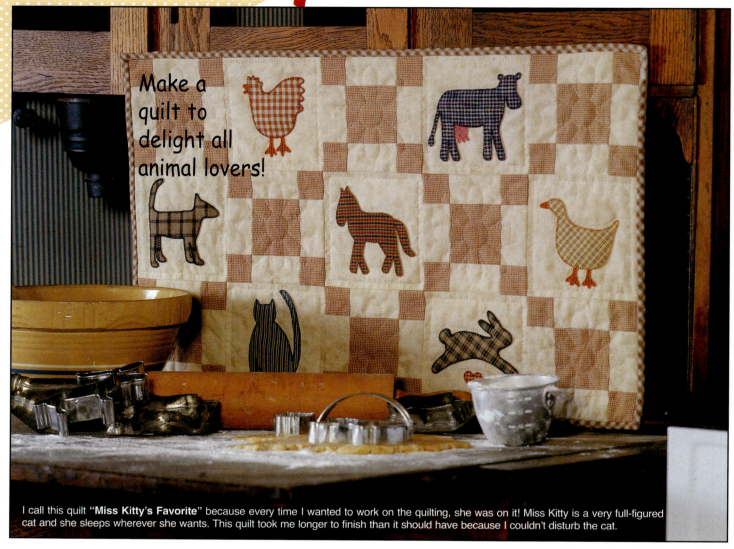

Make a quilt to delight all animal lovers!

I call this quilt **"Miss Kitty's Favorite"** because every time I wanted to work on the quilting, she was on it! Miss Kitty is a very full-figured cat and she sleeps wherever she wants. This quilt took me longer to finish than it should have because I couldn't disturb the cat.

QUILT SIZE: 25 1/2" x 15 1/2"
BLOCK SIZE: 5" square

MATERIALS
- 1/2 yard tea-dyed muslin (To tea dye fabric, see page 5.)
- Assorted homespun stripes, plaids, and checks for the animals
- Orange scrap for the beaks and feet
- Bright pink scrap for the cow's udder
- Red plaid scrap for the heart
- Fat quarter (18" x 22") light brown check homespun
- 1/2 yard light brown plaid homespun for the binding
- 27" x 17" piece of backing fabric
- 27" x 17" piece of thin batting
- Embroidery floss to match or contrast with the fabrics, including pink for the udder and orange for the beaks and feet
- Fusible Web

CUTTING
Trace the appropriate patterns (on pages 9 and 11) on the paper side of the fusible web, reversing the rabbit pattern. Cut the shapes out slightly beyond the lines. Fuse the shapes to the wrong side of the appropriate fabrics and cut them out on the lines.

For the appliqués:
- Cut 1 each: chicken, cow, dog, horse, duck, cat, and rabbit, assorted stripes, plaids, and checks
- Cut one of each beak and 4 feet, orange
- Cut 1: udder, bright pink
- Cut 1: heart, red plaid

Also:
- Cut 7: 6" squares, tea-dyed muslin
- Cut 32: 1 3/4" x 3" strips, tea-dyed muslin
- Cut 8: 3" squares, light brown check
- Cut 32: 1 3/4" squares, light brown check
- Cut 1 1/4"-wide bias strips, light brown plaid, to total 86" when joined for the binding

DIRECTIONS
- Center each animal on a 6" tea-dyed square. For the duck and

chicken, tuck the beak and feet under the edge of the body. For the cow, tuck the udder under the edge of the body. Place the heart below the rabbit as if the rabbit is jumping over it.
- Fuse the pieces to the squares.
- Stitch around the beaks, feet, and udder with a small blanket stitch using one strand of matching embroidery floss.
- Stitch around the animals using 2 strands of matching or contrasting embroidery floss.
- Press the blocks on the wrong side.
- Trim each block to 5 1/2" square, keeping the design centered.
- Stitch two 1 3/4" light brown check squares to a 1 3/4" x 3" tea-dyed muslin strip. Make 16.
- Stitch two 1 3/4" tea-dyed muslin strips to a 3" light brown check square. Make 8.
- Stitch the pieced strips to the remaining sides of the square to make a Puss-in-the-Corner block. Make 8.

Full-Size Patterns for Miss Kitty's Favorite
(More patterns on page 11.)

ASSEMBLY
- Referring to the quilt photo, lay out the Animal blocks and Puss-in-the-Corner blocks in 3 rows of 5.
- Stitch the blocks into rows and join the rows.
- Finish the quilt as described in the *General Directions*, using the 1 1/4"-wide light brown plaid bias strips and Binding Method #1.

NOTE: *Stitch the daisy quilting design (on page 32) on the Puss-in-the-Corner blocks for a country look.*

Summer Days

A rabbit running through wildflowers is a summer certainty.

Black-eyed Susans were my grandmother's favorite flower. She lived near a dirt road in the country with wild flowers growing everywhere, or so it seemed to me as a 5 year-old child. I picked lots and lots of them for her. **"Summer Days"** celebrates those hot days of playing in the country, picking flowers, and being thrilled to see a rabbit now and then.

QUILT SIZE: 15 1/4" x 8"

MATERIALS
- Fat eighth (11" x 18") blue print
- Tan print at least 3" x 4 1/2"
- 1/4 yard gold print
- Green print at least 3 1/2" x 6"
- Brown print scrap
- Blue with dots at least 2" x 15 1/4"
- 17" x 10" piece of backing fabric
- 17" x 10" piece of thin batting
- Embroidery floss to match or contrast with the fabrics
- Fusible Web

CUTTING
Trace the patterns on the paper side of the fusible web, reversing one of the flowers. Cut the shapes out slightly beyond the lines. Fuse the shapes to the wrong side of the appropriate fabrics and cut them out on the lines.
For the appliqués:
- Cut 1: rabbit, tan print
- Cut 2: stem/leaf pieces, green print
- Cut 2: flowers, gold print
- Cut 2: flower centers, brown print

Also:
- Cut 1: 13 1/4" x 6" rectangle, blue print
- Cut 2: 1 1/4" x 28" strips, gold print, for the binding

- Cut 2: 1 3/4" x 12 3/4" strips, gold print
- Cut 2: 1 3/4" x 8" strips, gold print
- Cut 2: 1" x 15 1/4" strips, blue with dots
- Cut 2: 1" x 8" strips, blue with dots

DIRECTIONS
- Fold the blue print rectangle in half crosswise. Lightly finger press the fold to mark the center.
- Center the rabbit on the rectangle, placing the bottom of the rabbit 1" from the bottom edge of the rectangle. Fuse it in place.
- Referring to the quilt photo, place the stem/leaf pieces on the rectangle, keeping them 1" from the bottom edge of the rectangle. Place the flowers and flower centers on the rectangle. Fuse them in place.
- Stitch around each piece with a small blanket stitch, using 2 strands of matching or contrasting embroidery floss.
- Press the quilt on the wrong side.
- Trim it to 12 3/4" x 5 1/2".
- Stitch the 1 3/4" x 12 3/4" gold print strips to the top and bottom of the quilt.
- Stitch the 1 3/4" x 8" gold print strips to the sides of the quilt.
- Press the blue dot strips in half lengthwise, right side out.
- Baste the 15 1/4" blue dot strips to the top and bottom of the quilt, aligning the raw edges and stitching a scant 1/4" from the edges.
- In the same manner, baste the 8" blue dot strips to the sides of the quilt.
- Finish the quilt as described in the *General Directions*, using the 1 1/4" x 28" gold print strips and binding Method #1.

Full-Size Pattern for Summer Days

Full-Size Pattern for Summer Days and Miss Kitty's Favorite

Full-Size Patterns for Miss Kitty's Favorite

11

Wild Things

Stitch perky little flowers to brighten your home.

I had to name this quilt **"Wild Things"** because, in terms of quilts, it's the wildest thing I've ever done! I tend to be conservative in my color choices but when I drew these flowers, I knew they had to be made with bright fabrics. It was such fun making this quilt and it has turned out to be one of my favorites.

QUILT SIZE: 13 1/2" x 19 1/2"
BLOCK SIZE: 5" square

MATERIALS
- 1/4 yard light mottled fabric for the block backgrounds
- 10 assorted bright prints, each at least 10" square
- 1/8 yard bright print for the binding
- 16" x 22" piece of backing fabric
- 16" x 22" piece of thin batting
- Embroidery floss to match or contrast with the fabrics
- Fusible Web

CUTTING
Trace the patterns on the paper side of the fusible web. Cut the shapes out slightly beyond the lines. Fuse the shapes to the wrong side of the appropriate fabrics and cut them out on the lines.
For the appliqués:
- Cut the flowers, flower centers, leaves, and stems from assorted bright prints. Refer to the photo, as necessary.

Also:
- Cut 6: 6" squares, light mottled background fabric
- Cut 4: 1" x 7" strips, assorted bright prints
- Cut 6: 1" x 6 1/2" strips, assorted bright prints
- Cut 24: 1" x 6" strips, assorted bright prints
- Cut 2: 1 1/4" x 20" strips, bright print, for the binding
- Cut 2: 1 1/4" x 15" strips, same bright print, for the binding

DIRECTIONS
- Arrange the pieces for each block on a background square in the following order: stem, leaves, flowers, and flower centers.
- Fuse the pieces in place.
- Stitch around each piece with a small blanket stitch, using 2 strands of matching or contrasting embroidery floss.
- Press the blocks on the wrong side.
- Trim each block to 5 1/2" square.
- Lay out the blocks in 3 rows of 2. Place a 1" x 6" bright print strip on each side of each block.
- Beginning with the first block, stitch the top strip to the top of the block, as shown, stopping about 1" from the end of the strip.

- Stitch the left strip to the block.

- Stitch the bottom strip to the block.
- Stitch the right strip to the block, keeping the end of the top strip out of the way.
- Finish stitching the top strip to the block. Place it back in the layout.
- Stitch the selected strips to the remaining blocks in the same manner.
- Stitch three 1" x 6 1/2" bright print strips together to make a side border. Make 2.
- Stitch them to the sides of the quilt, aligning the seams.
- Stitch two 1" x 7" bright print strips together to make a border. Make 2.
- Stitch them to the top and bottom of the quilt, aligning the seams.
- Finish the quilt as described in the *General Directions*, using the 1 1/4"-wide bright print strips and Binding Method #2.

Full-Size Patterns for Wild Things
(continued on page 15)

NOTE: *I outline quilted the flowers, leaves, and stems, and stitched in the ditch around the edge of each block. Diagonal lines 3/4" apart fill each block's background. Using a nickel for a pattern, I cut circles out of masking tape and quilted around them on the bright strips.*

Trio of Angels

Make these angels to watch over your family at Christmastime or anytime.

Do you need a quick gift or just want a holiday quilt that you can finish in a short period of time? *"Trio of Angels"* might be just what you're looking for. These three little angels in their simple setting will add quaint charm to your home.

QUILT SIZE: 15 1/2" x 7 1/2"

MATERIALS
- Beige print at least 6" x 14"
- Tan scrap at least 1 1/4" x 3" for the faces
- White print at least 4" x 9"
- Gold print at least 6" x 8"
- Green print at least 6" x 8"
- Red print at least 6" x 8"
- 1/8 yard green for the binding
- 17" x 9" piece of backing fabric
- 17" x 9" piece of thin batting
- Embroidery floss to match or contrast with the fabrics, including gold for the halos
- Fusible Web

CUTTING

Trace the patterns on the paper side of the fusible web. Cut the shapes out slightly beyond the lines. Fuse the shapes to the wrong side of the appropriate fabrics and cut them out on the lines.
For the appliqués:
- Cut 1: robe, each of red, green, and gold prints
- Cut 1: sleeve unit, each of red, green, and gold prints
- Cut 3 pairs of wings, white print
- Cut 3: faces, tan

Also:
- Cut 1: 6" x 14" rectangle, beige print
- Cut 40: 1 1/2" squares, gold, green, and red print
- Cut 2: 1 1/4" x 26" strips, green, for the binding

DIRECTIONS
- Fold the 6" x 14" beige print rectangle in half crosswise. Lightly finger press the fold to mark the center.
- Center one angel robe on the center fold, placing the bottom of the robe 3/4" from the bottom edge of the rectangle. Tuck the wings under the edges of the robe and place the sleeve unit on top. Fuse the pieces in place.
- Place the remaining angel wings, robes, and sleeve units on the background rectangle, leaving approximately 3/4" between the angels' wings. Fuse them in place.
- Place the faces on the background rectangle, just touching the angels' robes. Fuse them in place.
- Stitch around each piece with a small blanket stitch, using 2 strands of matching or contrasting embroidery floss.
- Using a pencil, draw an oval halo 3/16" above each angel face. Stitch the halos with a chain stitch, using 2 strands of gold embroidery floss.
- Press the appliquéd rectangle on the wrong side.
- Trim the rectangle to 13 1/2" x 5 1/2", keeping the design centered.
- Stitch thirteen 1 1/2" assorted red, green, and gold print squares together to make a long border. Make 2. Stitch them to the top and bottom of the quilt.
- Stitch seven 1 1/2" red, green, and gold print squares together to make a short border. Make 2. Stitch them to the sides of the quilt.
- Finish the quilt as described in the *General Directions*, using the 1 1/4" x 26" green strips and Binding Method #1.

NOTE: *The border quilting design I used for Trio of Angels is provided on page 15. Cut the shape out of paper. Align the straight edge of the paper with the inside edge of the border and trace the scalloped edge. Move the paper as necessary to continue the pattern.*

Christmas Pillows

Make these three little pillows just for fun!

"Christmas Pillows" are quick little projects to make. Tuck them in a basket, on a bench, or almost anywhere. They're great gifts, especially for a hostess or teacher.

PILLOW SIZE: 7" square
BLOCK SIZE: 5" square

MATERIALS
For the Angel Pillow:
- White print at least 6" square
- Red with dots at least 3" x 5 1/2"
- Gold print at least 4" square
- Green print at least 3 1/2" x 4"
- Tan scrap
- Green plaid at least 6" square
- Gold embroidery floss for the halo

For the Tree Pillow:
- Light polka dot at least 6" square
- Green print scrap
- Gold scrap
- Brown plaid scrap
- Red with dots at least 6" x 7 1/2"

For the Star Pillow:
- Green plaid at least 6" square
- Gold print, at least 4 1/2" square
- Red with dots at least 2 1/2" square
- Second gold print at least 6" x 7 1/2"

Also for each pillow:
- 9" square of muslin
- 9" square of backing fabric
- 9" square of thin batting
- Embroidery floss to match or contrast with the fabrics
- Polyester stuffing
- Fusible Web

CUTTING
Trace the patterns on the paper side of the fusible web. Cut the shapes out slightly beyond the lines. Fuse the shapes to the wrong side of the appropriate fabrics and cut them out on the lines.

For the Angel Pillow:
- Cut 1: 6" square, light print
- Cut 1: robe, red with dots
- Cut 4: 1 1/2" squares, red with dots
- Cut 1 pair: angel wings, gold print
- Cut 1: sleeve unit, green print
- Cut 1: face, tan
- Cut 4: 1 1/2" x 5 1/2" strips, green plaid

For the Tree Pillow:
- Cut 1: 6" square, light polka dot
- Cut 1: tree, green print
- Cut 1: star, gold print
- Cut 1: tree trunk, brown plaid
- Cut 2: 1 1/2" x 5 1/2" strips, red with dots
- Cut 2: 1 1/2" x 7 1/2" strips, red with dots

For the Star Pillow:
- Cut 1: 6" square, green plaid
- Cut 1: large star, gold print
- Cut 1: small star, red with dots
- Cut 2: 1 1/2" x 5 1/2" strips, gold print
- Cut 2: 1 1/2" x 7 1/2" strips, gold print

DIRECTIONS
For the Angel Pillow:
- Place the pieces on the 6" white print square in this order: wings, robe, sleeve unit, and face. Place the bottom of the robe 3/4" from the bottom of the square. Measure the sides and adjust the arrangement as necessary to keep it centered.
- Fuse the pieces in place.
- Stitch around each piece with a small blanket stitch, using 2 strands of matching or contrasting embroidery floss.
- Using a pencil, draw an oval halo 3/16" above the angel's face. Stitch the halo with a chain stitch, using 2 strands of gold embroidery floss.
- Press the block on the wrong side.
- Trim the block to 5 1/2" square, keeping the angel centered.
- Stitch 1 1/2" x 5 1/2" green plaid strips to the top and bottom of the angel block.
- Stitch 1 1/2" red squares to the ends of the remaining 1 1/2" x 5 1/2" green plaid strips. Stitch them to the sides of the block.

For the Tree Pillow:
- Place the tree on the 6" light polka dot square. Tuck the trunk under the bottom of the tree. Place the gold star on the top. Measure the sides, top, and bottom and adjust the arrangement as necessary to keep it centered.
- Fuse the pieces in place.
- Stitch around the trunk and star with a small blanket stitch, using one strand of matching or contrasting embroidery floss.
- Stitch around the tree using 2 strands of matching or contrasting embroidery floss.
- Press the block on the wrong side.
- Trim the block to 5 1/2" square, keeping the tree centered.
- Stitch the 1 1/2" x 5 1/2" red strips to the sides of the tree block. Stitch the 1 1/2" x 7 1/2" red strips to the top and bottom.

For the Star Pillow:
- Center the large gold print star and the small red star on the 6" green plaid square.
- Fuse the pieces in place.
- Stitch around each piece with a small blanket stitch, using 2 strands of matching or contrasting embroidery floss.
- Press the block on the wrong side.
- Trim the block to 5 1/2" square, keeping the stars centered.
- Stitch the 1 1/2" x 5 1/2" gold print strips to opposite sides of the star block. Stitch the 1 1/2" x 7 1/2" gold print strips to the remaining sides.

FINISHING
- Layer a 9" muslin square, batting, and pillow top, right side up. Baste the layers. Quilt as desired.
- Trim the batting and muslin even with the edge of the pillow top.
- Place the pillow top on the 9" backing fabric square, right sides together. Pin the layers. Stitch around the outside edge of the pillow top 1/4" from the edge, and leave a 3" opening on the bottom for turning. Trim the backing even with the edge of the pillow top.
- Turn the pillow right side out and stuff with polyester stuffing.
- Slipstitch the opening closed.

Full-Size Pattern for Christmas Pillows

(More Patterns on page 15)

Checkers Anyone?

Make a quilt they'll enjoy time after time.

Besides being a fun game, **"Checkers Anyone?"** makes a great table runner. Place it in the middle of your dining table or on an end table with the pieces close by, and watch how often your family will play. It's one game you won't have to make them put away!

QUILT SIZE: 23" x 14"

MATERIALS
- 1/4 yard gold with dots
- 1/4 yard red plaid
- 1/4 yard green with dots
- 25" x 16" piece of backing fabric
- 25" x 16" piece of thin batting
- Embroidery floss to match or contrast with the fabrics, including gold for the windows
- Twenty-four 1 1/4" unfinished wooden checkers
- Green and red craft paint
- Spray acrylic sealer
- Fusible Web

CUTTING
Trace the patterns (here and on page 22) on the paper side of the fusible web. Cut the shapes out slightly beyond the lines. Fuse the shapes to the wrong side of the appropriate fabrics and cut them out on the lines.

For the appliqués:
- Cut 16: windows, gold with dots
- Cut 3: houses, red plaid
- Cut 3: doors, red plaid
- Cut 3: roofs, red plaid
- Cut 3: houses, green with dots
- Cut 3: doors, green with dots
- Cut 3: roofs, green with dots
- Cut 4: trees, green with dots

Also:
- Cut 4: 2" x 18" strips, gold with dots
- Cut 2: 5 1/2" x 15" rectangles, gold with dots
- Cut 4: 2" x 18" strips, red plaid

Full-Size Pattern for Checkers Anyone?

18

- Cut 2: 1 1/4" x 14" strips, green with dots
- Cut 2: 1 1/4" x 12 1/2" strips, green with dots
- Cut 2: 1 1/4" x 44" strips, green with dots, for the binding

DIRECTIONS

- Place a 2" x 18" gold strip on a 2" x 18" red strip, right sides together, and stitch them together along one long side. Make 4.
- Place a strip pair on another strip pair, alternating gold and red, and stitch them together keeping the red strip on top as you stitch. Sew the remaining pairs to this unit in the same manner. Press the seam allowances in one direction.
- Cut eight 2" sections from the pieced panel, as shown.

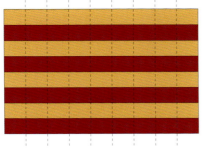

- Sew the sections together along their long sides, alternating gold and red. Press the seam allowances open.
- Stitch the 1 1/4" x 12 1/2" green strips to opposite sides of the checkerboard.
- Stitch the 1 1/4" x 14" green strips to the remaining sides of the checkerboard. Set it aside.

For the Checkers:
- Paint 12 of the unfinished checkers with red paint and 12 with green.
- When the paint is completely dry, spray them with clear acrylic sealer.

- Fold a 5 1/2" x 15" gold rectangle in half crosswise. Lightly finger press the fold to mark the center.
- Arrange a green house and a red roof on the center fold of the rectangle, keeping them an equal distance from the top and bottom. Place two windows and a red door on the house.

- Fuse the pieces in place.
- Referring to the photo, arrange the remaining green houses and red roofs on the rectangle, placing them 2 1/4" from the center house. Place a red door and 3 windows on each of those houses. Fuse them in place.
- Center 2 trees between the houses and fuse them in place.
- Stitch around the windows with a small blanket stitch, using one strand of matching embroidery floss.
- Stitch around the remaining pieces using 2 strands of matching or contrasting embroidery floss.
- Stitch the red houses, green roofs, green doors, and the remaining windows and trees to the second 5 1/2" x 15" gold rectangle in the same manner.
- Press the rectangles on the wrong side.
- Trim them to 5" x 14", keeping the appliqué designs centered.
- Stitch the appliquéd rectangles to opposite sides of the checkerboard.
- Finish the quilt as described in the *General Directions*, using the 1 1/4" x 44" green strips and Binding Method #1.

Checkers Pouch

Keep your checkers all wrapped up so they won't get lost.

MATERIALS
- Gold with dots at least 8 1/2" x 12"
- Red plaid at least 8" x 15"

CUTTING
- Cut 2: 6" x 8 1/2" rectangles, gold with dots
- Cut 1: 6" x 11 1/2" rectangle, red plaid
- Cut 2: 1" x 16" strips, red plaid
- Loop turner

DIRECTIONS

- Place the 6" x 8 1/2" gold rectangles right sides together. Stitch both long sides and one short side, backstitching at the beginning and at the end. Turn it right side out.

- Fold a 1" x 16" red plaid strip in half lengthwise, right side in. Stitch along the length with a 1/4" seam allowance, backstitching at each end. Trim the seam allowance to 1/8". Using a loop turner, turn the sewn strip right side out. Make 2.
- Pin the ties in the center of one side of the gold bag, aligning one end of each tie with the raw edge of the bag.
- Fold the red plaid rectangle in half crosswise, right side in. Stitch the ends of the rectangle together to form a tube, back-

(continued on page 23)

Folk Art Sampler

Use ticking stripes for a country look.

Making samplers is fun because you get to make a variety of blocks. I can hardly wait to finish one so I can start the next. **"Folk Art Sampler"** (17" x 23") and **"Folk Art in Plaid"** (21 3/4" x 14 1/2") began as a block series for *Miniature Quilts* magazine. I enjoyed making them so much that I just had to design more.

Folk Art in Plaid

Use a simple setting for on-point blocks.

Folk Art Sampler

QUILT SIZE: 17" x 23"
BLOCK SIZE: 5" square

MATERIALS

- 6 assorted blue prints, each at least 6" square
- Assorted prints for the appliqués
- Scrap of cotton batting at least 3" x 5" for the sheep
- 1/4 yard red print
- 1/8 yard blue ticking
- 1/4 yard dark blue print
- 19" x 25" piece of backing fabric
- 19" x 25" piece of thin batting
- Embroidery floss to match or contrast with the fabrics, including orange and black for the bird
- Fusible Web

CUTTING

Trace the patterns (on pages 22 and 23 and the sheep pattern on page 5) on the paper side of the fusible web. Cut the shapes out slightly beyond the lines. Fuse the shapes to the wrong side of the appropriate fabrics and cut them out on the lines.

For the appliqués:

- Cut the pieces for each block from assorted prints. Refer to the photo, as necessary. NOTE: *For the sheep, refer to Fusing Cotton Batting, on page 22.*

Also:

- Cut 6: 6" squares, assorted blue prints
- Cut 2: 1 1/4" x 44" strips, red print, for the binding
- Cut 12: 1 1/2" squares, red print
- Cut 17: 1 1/2" x 5 1/2" crosswise strips, blue ticking
- Cut 4: 2 1/4" x 21" strips, dark blue print

DIRECTIONS

- Referring to the photo, arrange the pieces for one block on a 6" blue print square, keeping all the pieces at least 3/4" from the edges.
- Fuse the pieces in place. In the same manner, arrange and fuse the pieces on the 5 remaining blocks.
- Stitch around each piece with a small blanket stitch, using 2 strands of matching or contrasting embroidery floss. For small pieces like the stars and windows, use one strand of floss.
- For the bird, use one strand of black embroidery floss and an outline stitch to embroider the wing and tail feathers. Using 2 strands of black floss wrapped twice around the needle, make a French Knot for the bird's eye. Using 2 strands of orange embroidery floss, embroider the beak with a satin stitch. Stitch the bird's legs with a straight stitch.
- Press the blocks on the wrong side.
- Trim each block to 5 1/2" square.
- Referring to the quilt photo, lay out the blocks in 3 rows of 2. Place the 1 1/2" x 5 1/2" ticking strips and 1 1/2" red print squares in the layout.

(continued on page 22)

Folk Art in Plaid

QUILT SIZE: 21 3/4" x 14 1/2"
BLOCK SIZE: 5" square

MATERIALS

- 6 assorted light plaid and stripe fabrics, each at least 6" square
- Assorted prints for the appliqués
- Scrap of cotton batting at least 3" x 5" for the sheep
- 12 assorted medium and dark plaids, each at least 4 1/2" square
- 1/8 yard navy for the binding
- 24" x 17" piece of backing fabric
- 24" x 17" piece of thin batting
- Embroidery floss to match or contrast with the fabrics, including orange and black for the bird
- Fusible Web

CUTTING

Trace the patterns (on pages 22 and 23 and the sheep pattern on page 5) on the paper side of the fusible web. Cut the shapes out slightly beyond the lines. Fuse the shapes to the wrong side of the appropriate fabrics and cut them out on the lines.

For the appliqués:

- Cut the pieces for each block from assorted prints. Refer to the photo, as necessary. NOTE: *For the sheep, refer to Fusing Cotton Batting, on page 22.*

Also:

- Cut 6: 6" squares, assorted light plaids and stripes
- Cut 12: 4 1/2" squares, assorted medium and dark plaids, then cut them in half diagonally to yield 24 triangles
- Cut 2: 1 1/4" x 44" strips, navy, for the binding

DIRECTIONS

- Referring to the photo, arrange the pieces for one block diagonally on a 6" light plaid or stripe square, keeping all the pieces at least 3/4" from the edges.
- Fuse the pieces in place. In the same manner, arrange and fuse the pieces on the 5 remaining blocks.
- Stitch around each piece with a small blanket stitch, using 2 strands of matching or contrasting embroidery floss. For small pieces like the stars and windows, use one strand of floss.
- For the bird, use one strand of black embroidery floss and an outline stitch to embroider the wing and tail feathers. Using 2 strands of black floss wrapped twice around the needle, make a French Knot for the bird's eye. Using 2 strands of orange embroidery floss, embroider the beak with a satin stitch. Stitch the bird's legs with a straight stitch.
- Press the blocks on the wrong side.
- Trim each block to 5 1/2" square.
- Referring to the quilt photo, lay out the blocks, on point, and the 24 plaid triangles. Rearrange the blocks and triangles until you like their placement.

(continued on page 22)

Folk Art Sampler

- Stitch the red print squares and horizontal ticking strips into 4 sashing rows.
- Stitch the blocks and vertical ticking strips into 3 rows.
- Join the block rows and sashing rows.
- Measure the length of the quilt. Trim 2 of the 2 1/4" x 21" dark blue print strips to that measurement. Stitch them to the sides of the quilt.
- Measure the width of the quilt. Trim the remaining 2 1/4" x 21" dark blue print strips to that measurement. Stitch them to the top and bottom of the quilt.
- Finish the quilt according to the *General Directions*, using the 1 1/4" x 44" red print strips and Binding Method #1.

NOTE: *I outline quilted all of the appliqué shapes, stitched in-the-ditch around the blocks, sashing strips, and cornerstones, quilted an X in each cornerstone, and quilted Stars on the border.*

Full-Size Patterns for Folk Art Sampler and Folk Art in Plaid

Folk Art in Plaid

- Starting with the first block, stitch a triangle to each side to make a Square-in-a-square unit.
- Return the unit to the layout and repeat for each remaining block.
- Stitch the blocks into 3 vertical rows. Join the rows.
- Finish the quilt according to the *General Directions*, using the 1 1/4" x 44" navy strips and Binding Method #1.

Fusing Cotton Batting

- Trace the sheep pattern on page 5 on the fusible web.
- In preparation for fusing cotton batting, lightly press the batting in the following way: Using steam, hold the iron just above the batting, barely touching it with the iron. The steam will shrink the batting slightly.
- Using a light touch, press the fusible web to the wrong side of the batting. Press just long enough to fuse it. Let it cool and cut out the shape.
- Remove the paper and place the fused shape on the right side of the background fabric. Pin it in one or 2 places to hold it in place.
- Turn the fabric over, wrong side up. Lightly press to hold the shape in place, avoiding the pins. Remove the pins and press the remaining areas.

Full-Size House Pattern also for Checkers Anyone?

Full-Size Patterns for Folk Art Sampler and Folk Art in Plaid

Checkers Pouch <small>(continued from page 19)</small>

stitching at each end. Press the seam allowance open. Press one edge of the tube 1/4" toward the wrong side.

- Place the gold bag inside the red tube, right sides together, aligning the raw edges. Align the seamline of the tube with one seamline of the gold bag. Stitch them together along the raw edge, enclosing the ends of the ties in the seam. Press the seam allowance toward the red plaid.
- Fold the red tube in half toward the inside of the gold bag. Pin the pressed edge to the bag covering the seamline. Hand stitch it in place or machine stitch it in the following way: With the bag right side out, fold the red tube toward the inside so the pressed edge extends about 1/16" below the stitching line. Pin it in place from the outside. Machine stitch in the ditch of the seam, keeping the ties out of the way.
- Place the checkers in the pouch. Fold it in thirds with the red band and the ties on the outside. Wrap one tie around the pouch and bring the other toward the pouch top. Tie them in a bow and trim the ends, as desired. Tie a knot at the end of each tie.

NOTE: *After trimming the ties, one will be longer than the other. Wrap the long one underneath the pouch and tie it on top with the shorter one.*

Caitie's Cats

Won't you please give these three little kitties a home?

My daughter Caitlin made **"Caitie's Cats"** simply because she loves cats! We have 2 adopted strays but Caitie still begs for more. Very often while I'm driving, I hear "Mom, STOP, there's a kitty!" "Can we keep him?" and "Oh, can we feed him?" are 2 other often used phrases around our house. If you love cats as much as we do, you'll want to make at least one little cat quilt.

QUILT SIZE: 9" x 24"
BLOCK SIZE: 5" square

MATERIALS
- Piece of muslin at least 6" x 18"
- 3 polka dot scraps, each at least 5" square, for the cats
- 1/8 yard light polka dot
- 1/4 yard brown polka dot
- 11" x 26" piece of backing fabric
- 11" x 26" piece of thin batting
- Embroidery floss to match or contrast with the fabrics
- Fusible Web

CUTTING
Trace the patterns on the paper side of the fusible web. Cut the shapes out slightly beyond the lines. Fuse the shapes to the wrong side of the appropriate fabrics and cut them out on the lines.
For the appliqués:
- Cut 1: cat from each polka dot scrap
Also:
- Cut 3: 6" squares, muslin
- Cut 2: 1 1/2" x 23" strips, light polka dot
- Cut 2: 1 1/2" x 10" strips, light polka dot
- Cut 2: 1 1/2" x 7" strips, light polka dot
- Cut 2: 1 1/4" x 44" strips, brown polka dot, for the binding

- Cut 6: 1 1/4" x 5 1/2" strips, brown polka dot
- Cut 6: 1 1/4" x 7" strips, brown polka dot

DIRECTIONS
- Center and fuse a cat on each 6" muslin square.
- Stitch around each cat with a small blanket stitch, using 2 strands of matching or contrasting embroidery floss.
- Press the blocks on the wrong side.
- Trim each block to 5 1/2" square, keeping the cat centered.
- Stitch 1 1/4" x 5 1/2" brown polka dot strips to the sides of each block.
- Stitch 1 1/4" x 7" brown polka dot strips to the top and bottom of each block.
- Referring to the quilt photo, lay out the blocks with the 1 1/2" x 7" light polka dot strips between them. Stitch the blocks and strips together.
- Measure the length of the quilt. Trim the 1 1/2" x 23" light polka dot strips to that measurement and stitch them to the sides of the quilt.
- Measure the width of the quilt. Trim the 1 1/2" x 10" light polka dot strips to that measurement and stitch them to the top and bottom of the quilt.
- Finish the quilt as described in the *General Directions*, using the 1 1/4" x 44" brown polka dot strips and Binding Method #1.

Full-Size Patterns for Caitie's Cats

Old Cat

Stitch a replica of a well-loved toy.

My dear friend Andrea bought this grumpy-looking gentleman on one of our antique expeditions in Connecticut. Knowing that I liked **"Old Cat"** so much, Andrea gave him to me when I moved back to Pennsylvania 12 years ago. He continues to be a treasured gift.

MATERIALS
- Piece of muslin at least 7" x 12"
- 1/2 yard tan flannel
- 6" square of green felt
- 1/3 yard off-white flannel
- 12" square of red felt
- Polyester stuffing
- 2 glass eyes or buttons
- Black perle cotton
- 20" length of 1/8" cord or ribbon
- 6" piece of ribbon (optional)

CUTTING
Pattern pieces (on pages 28-30) are full size and include a 1/4" seam allowance.
For the Cat:
- Cut 2: body pieces, muslin
- Cut 2: legs, tan flannel
- Cut 2: foot pads, green felt
- Cut 2: arm backs, tan flannel
- Cut 2: hand pads, green felt
- Cut 2: arm fronts, tan flannel
- Cut 2: head fronts, tan flannel, reversing one
- Cut 2: head backs, tan flannel, reversing one

For the clothes:
- Cut 1: jumpsuit, off-white flannel (Fold an 11" x 22" piece of flannel in quarters and place the two edges of the pattern on the folds as indicated on the pattern.)
- Cut 1: 3/4" x 14" bias strip, muslin
- Cut 1: 1" x 8 1/2" strip, muslin
- Cut 1: jacket back, red felt
- Cut 2: jacket fronts, red felt
- Cut 2: 3" x 6 1/2" rectangles, red felt, for the sleeves
- Cut 1: pocket, red felt
- Cut 1: pocket, green felt (optional)

DIRECTIONS
- Fold each body piece in half, right side in. Sew the darts, as shown.

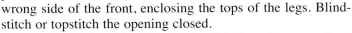

- Place the head fronts right sides together. Sew the center front seam. Place the head backs right sides together and sew the center back seam.
- Place the head front and head back right sides together and sew around the outside. Clip the seam allowance at the inner corner of the ear, as indicated on the pattern. Turn the head right side out. Place a tiny amount of stuffing in each ear. Lay the head flat and stitch across the bottom of each ear, backstitching at each end.

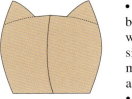

- Sew a hand pad to an arm front. Sew the pieced arm front to the arm back, right sides together, leaving the top open. Make 2.
- Fold a leg piece in half right side in, and sew the front seam, leaving the top and bottom of each leg open. Make 2.
- Fold a foot pad in half lengthwise and mark the fold in the seam allowance at each end. Pin a leg to a foot pad, right sides together, matching the seamlines of the leg with the marks on the footpad. Sew them together, aligning the edges as you stitch.

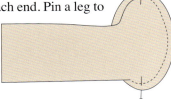

- Stuff the arms and legs firmly to within 1" of the tops.

TIP: *Place a pin across the piece through both layers, 1" from the top, to keep the stuffing from pushing out.*

- Place the arms on the right side of one body piece, fronts down, 3/4" from the top. Baste them in place. Place the legs on the bottom of the same body piece, fronts down, and baste them in place.

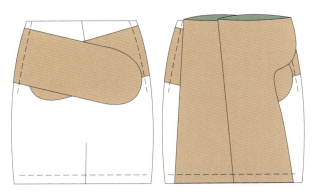

- Keeping the arms toward the body but the legs extending down, pin the body pieces right sides together. Sew the side seams. You may have to manipulate the arms to keep the edges straight as you stitch.
- Tuck the head down inside the body so it's right sides together with the body front, aligning the side seams. Be sure the fronts match. Pin them together. Sew around the neck seam twice.
- Turn the cat right side out. Stuff the head and body firmly. Turn the bottom edge of the back body piece under 1/4" and pin it to the wrong side of the front, enclosing the tops of the legs. Blindstitch or topstitch the opening closed.
- Thread a needle with a 15" length of black perle cotton. Knot the end.
- Insert the needle into the nose area (near point D) of the face, bringing it back out at point A. Pop the knot through the fabric and tug on the floss to bury the knot inside the stuffing. Insert the needle at point B, and bring it back out at point C, catching the first stitch. Pull the perle cotton just until the stitch lies flat on the face and makes an inverted V. Insert the needle at point D and bring it back up at E.

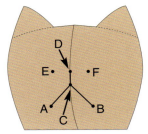

- Stitch the nose using a satin stitch, starting at E and moving to F. When you get to the last stitch, make a knot one stitch length away from the where the perle cotton comes out of the fabric. Insert the needle and bring it back up 1" away from the point of entry. Tug on the floss to pull the knot through the fabric. Cut the excess floss at the surface of the cat.

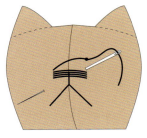

- Sew the eyes in place.

For the Jumpsuit:
- Make a 3 3/4" cut down the center at the top edge of one section of the jumpsuit (this will be the back).

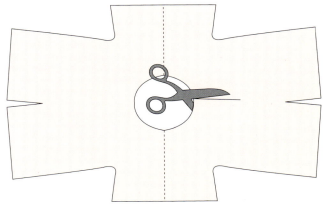

- Place the cut edge of the jumpsuit on the 1" x 8 1/2" muslin strip, right sides together. Sew them together, maintaining a 1/4" seam allowance on the muslin strip but tapering the jumpsuit to the end of the cut, as shown. Trim the end of the muslin strip even with the jumpsuit.
- Fold the remaining edge of the muslin strip 1/4" toward the inside. Fold the strip again, enclosing the raw edges. Sew the folded edge in place along the stitching line.
- Press one long edge of the 3/4" x 14" muslin bias strip toward the wrong side.
- Leaving 1/4" extending beyond the edge of the jumpsuit, sew the bias strip to the neck edge, right sides together. Trim the end of the strip, leaving a 1/4" allowance.
- Press the muslin strip toward the inside of the jumpsuit. Turn the ends under, and topstitch along the folded edge, leaving the ends open.
- Press the sleeve and leg edges 1/4" toward the wrong side. Press them 1/4" again to make a hem. Do not sew them yet.
- Fold the jumpsuit in half, right side in, at the shoulders. Open the pressed hems and sew the side/underarm seams. Sew the inside leg seam. Turn the jumpsuit right side out.
- Turn each pressed hem toward the inside and topstitch along the fold.
- Run the 20" of cord or ribbon through the neck casing.
- Tie the 6" length of ribbon in a little bow and trim the ends. Attach the bow to the front neckline of the jumpsuit, if desired.

For the Jacket:
- Place the front pieces on the back piece, right sides together. Sew the shoulder seams.

- Sew a 3" x 6 1/2" rectangle into each armhole.
- Sew the underarm seams from the bottom of the sleeves to the bottom of the jacket. Turn it right side out.
- Fold each lapel on the dotted line and topstitch the edge to the jacket front.

- Optional: Trim 1/8" away from the edge of the green felt pocket and stitch or glue it on the red pocket. Pin the red felt pocket to the right side jacket front and topstitch it in place close to the edge.
- Turn up the bottom of each sleeve to make a 1/2" cuff.

Full-Size Patterns for Old Cat

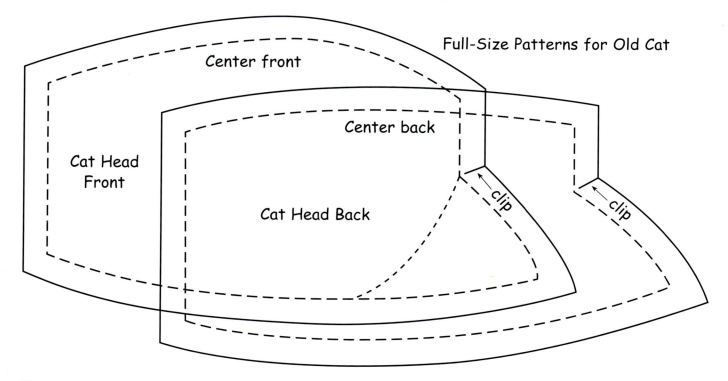

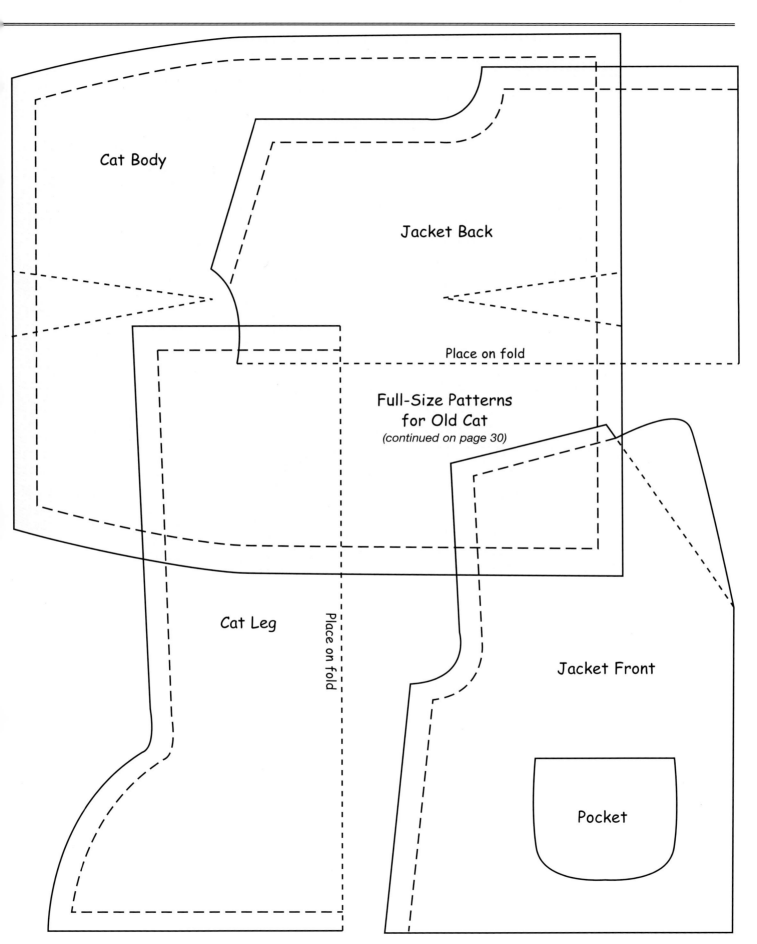

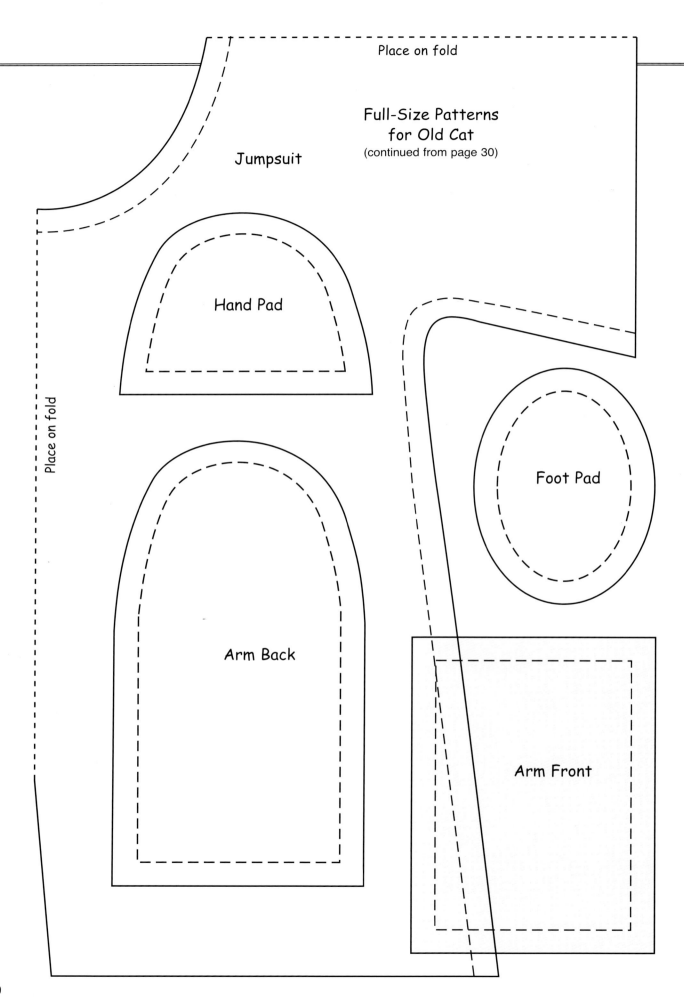

General Directions

About the Patterns

Read through the pattern directions before cutting fabric for the project. Pattern directions are given in step-by-step order. Pattern pieces for fusible web appliqué are full size and do not include a turn-under allowance. All other dimensions include a 1/4" seam allowance.

Fabric

I recommend using 100% cotton fabrics. Test all of your fabrics to be sure they are colorfast. I suggest washing your fabrics before using them. Yardage is based on 44" fabric with a useable width of 42".

Fusible Web

For larger appliqués, especially if they will have other appliqués fused on top of them, I trim the center from the cut fusible web piece before adhering it to the fabric. This reduces bulk and stiffness in the finished quilt. For example, for a flower that will have a center fused on top of it, trace the flower on the fusible web. Cut it out about 1/8" to 1/4" outside the line. Then cut 1/4" away from the line on the inside. Either discard the center or use it for another appliqué piece.

Fuse the trimmed flower outline to the fabric and cut the flower out on the line. Fuse the flower to the desired fabric according to the manufacturer's directions.

Marking Fabric

Test all marking tools for removability before using them. I suggest using silver or white marking tools for dark fabrics and fine line pencils for light fabrics. Always use a sharp pencil and a light touch. Lay a piece of fine-grained sandpaper under the fabric to keep it from slipping while you mark it, if desired.

Machine Sewing

To make a stitching guide: Cut a length of masking tape or moleskin foot pad about 1/4" x 2". Place a clear plastic ruler under the presser foot to the left of the needle. Slowly slide the ruler to the right until the needle is aligned with the 1/4" mark on the ruler. Lower the presser foot to hold the ruler in place. Carefully adhere the moleskin on the throat plate along the right edge of the ruler. Feed fabric under the needle, touching this guide.

Set the stitch length to 12 stitches per inch. Stitch pieces together, from edge to edge unless directed to do otherwise in the pattern.

Pressing

Press seams toward the darker of the two fabrics unless otherwise noted. Press abutting seams in opposite directions whenever possible. Use a dry iron and press carefully, as little pieces are easy to distort.

Squaring Blocks

To square the 5" blocks and make it easier to keep the design centered, I made a paper frame. Cut a 7" square of paper. Draw a centered 5 1/2" square (includes seam allowances) on the paper square and cut it out, leaving a frame.

Place the frame on the block to be squared. Center the design as desired and make 2 small marks in each corner of the cut-out square. Align a ruler with the marks and use a rotary cutter to trim the edges of the block.

 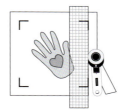

FINISHING
Marking Quilting Designs

Simple designs can be cut from adhesive-backed shelf paper or masking tape. They'll stick and re-stick several times. Masking tape can also be used to mark grids. Remove the tape when you're not quilting to avoid leaving a sticky residue. Mark lightly with pencils; thick lines that won't go away really stand out on a small quilt.

I often cut shapes out of paper then trace around them with a mechanical pencil or white quilt marking pencil.

Batting

Use a low-loft or very thin batting. My favorites are Quilter's Dream Cotton (Request loft) by Kelsul and Thermore by Hobbs. Layer the quilt sandwich as follows: backing, wrong side up; batting; quilt top, right side up. Baste or pin the layers together. In addition, I always baste around the perimeter of the quilt, about 3/16" from the edge. There is no need to remove these basting stitches as they will be covered by the binding.

Quilting

Very small quilts can be lap-quilted without a hoop. Larger ones can be quilted in a hoop or small frame. Use a short, thin needle (between) and small stitches that will be in scale with the little quilt. Thread the needle with a single strand of thread and knot one end. Insert the needle through the quilt top and batting (not the backing) 1/2" away from where you want to begin quilting. Gently pull the thread to pop the knot through the top and bury it in the batting. Quilt as desired.

Binding
Method #1:

For most straight-edged miniature quilts, a single-fold binding is an attractive, durable, and easy finish. NOTE: *If your quilt has curved or scalloped edges, binding strips must be cut on the bias of the fabric.* Cut binding strips 1 1/4" wide. Sew the strips together with diagonal seams; trim and press the seams open.

Trim one end of the strip at a 45° angle. Press one long edge of the binding strip 1/4" toward the wrong side. Starting with the trimmed end, position the binding strip, right sides together, on the quilt top, aligning the raw edge of the binding with the bottom edge of the quilt top. Leaving approximately 2" of the binding strip free, and beginning at least 3 inches from one corner, stitch the binding to the quilt with a 1/4" seam allowance, measuring from the edge of the binding and quilt top.

When you reach a corner, stop the stitching line exactly 1/4" from the edge of the quilt top. Backstitch, clip threads, and remove the quilt from the machine. Fold the binding up and away, creating a 45° angle, as shown.

Fold the binding down as shown, and begin stitching at the edge.

Continue stitching around the quilt to within 2" of the starting point. Lay the binding flat against the quilt, overlapping the beginning end. Open the pressed edge on each end and fold the end of the binding at a 45° angle against the angle on the beginning end of the binding. Finger press the fold.

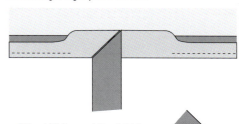

Trim 1/2" beyond the fold line. Place the ends of the binding right sides together and stitch with a 1/4" seam allowance. Finger press the seam allowance open.

Place the binding flat against the quilt and finish stitching it to the quilt. Trim the batting and backing even with the edge of the quilt top. Fold the binding to the back of the quilt, and blindstitch it to the back, covering the seamline.

Method #2:

Press one long edge of each binding strip 1/4" toward the wrong side. Center a pressed strip on one side of the quilt, right sides together, aligning the raw edges. Stitch the strip to the quilt with a 1/4" seam allowance. Trim the binding ends even with the edge of the quilt.

Trim the backing and batting even with the edge of the quilt along that side. Fold the binding over the edge of the quilt and blindstitch the folded edge to the back, covering the stitching line. Repeat for the opposite side of the quilt.